CW00521410

ISBN: 9798379212575

Imprint: Independently published

Contents Page

Introduction

Welcome to the Manchester United Biographies for Kids. I hope you're raring to learn about 25 legends of this amazing football club!

Each player's biography will start with a full-size image so that you are able to recognise them in future if you don't already! This will be followed by two pages of information starting with a few stats which are date of birth, year of United debut, nationality, position, height and major trophies won during their time at the club (including Charity Shields and Super Cups).

Next, you'll get an overview of their early career, late career, accomplishments and a summary with a particular focus on their Old Trafford careers. Enjoy!

The Stretford End being demolished in 1992 after the Taylor report made it a legal requirement that all First Division stadiums be converted into all-seaters following the Hillsborough disaster.

Trophy Cabinet

First Division/Premier League (20; Record)

1907–08, 1910–11, 1951–52, 1955–56, 1956–57, 1964–65, 1966–67, 1992–93, 1993–94, 1995–96, 1996–97, 1998–99, 1999–2000, 2000–01, 2002–03, 2006–07, 2007–08, 2008–09, 2010–11, 2012–13

Second Division (2)

1935–36, 1974–75

FA Cup (12)

1908–09, 1947–48, 1962–63, 1976–77, 1982–83, 1984–85, 1989–90, 1993–94, 1995–96, 1998–99, 2003–04, 2015–16

League Cup (6)

1991–92, 2005–06, 2008–09, 2009–10, 2016–17, 2022-23

Charity Shield (21; Record)

1908, 1911, 1952, 1956, 1957, 1965*, 1967*, 1977*, 1983, 1990*, 1993, 1994, 1996, 1997, 2003, 2007, 2008, 2010, 2011, 2013, 2016 (* shared)

European Cup/Champions League (3)

1967–68, 1998–99, 2007–08

Europa League (1)

2016–17

UEFA Super Cup (1)

1991

Intercontinental Cup/FIFA Club World Cup (2)

1999, 2008

UEFA Cup Winners' Cup (1)

1990/91

DAVID BECKHAM

Born: 2nd May 1975
United Debut: 1992
Nationality: English
Position: Right Midfielder
Height: 5 ft 11 in (1.80 m)
Major Trophies: 12

Early Career

David Robert Joseph Beckham was born in Leytonstone, East London. His ambition was to be a football player when at school. Both his parents were avid United supporters and they frequently travelled 200 miles (320 km) to Old Trafford from London to attend home matches. He was signed by his boyhood club as a schoolboy on his 14th birthday. Beckham made his senior team debut in September 1992 and became a professional four months later. In December 1994, on his Champions League debut, he netted a goal against Galatasaray, and a first Premier League outing followed in April 1995 against Leeds. He was part of a young group of players, known as "The Class of '92", who would become top players in the years to come. He had a short loan spell with Preston North End in 1995 where he scored two goals in five appearances including a goal directly from a corner.

Later Career

In the 1995/96 campaign, he was instrumental in the FA Cup success, scoring the winner in the semi-final win and then providing the corner for the winning goal in the final. The club also won the league title that season. He received instant recognition in August 1996, with a goal against Wimbledon when he scored from the halfway line, around 57 yards out. He provided the most assists with 13 in the 1997/98 league campaign. The next season, he won the treble of league, FA Cup and Champions League, including a crucial goal in the final league game as United clinched the title and then provided two goal scoring corners in the 1999 Champions League Final. United easily won the league title in 1999/2000 by 18 points, with Beckham netting five times as the club won their final 11 league games. The 2001/02 season saw him record a career-best 16 goals in a season. He moved to Spanish side Real Madrid a year later, where he scored a goal in under three minutes on his league debut. He won the League title once in his four seasons there. He then made a shock move to LA Galaxy of the MLS where he won two league titles in six seasons and helped to revolutionise the sport in America. The final game of his career came with Paris Saint-Germain in May 2013, after two loan spells at AC Milan.

Accomplishments

Beckham played a total of 394 games for United and scored 85 times. He appeared in over 700 competitive games during his career. With United, he won the league title six times, the Champions League once, and the FA Cup twice. He also won one league title each with Real Madrid and Paris Saint-Germain. He was the first British footballer to play in 100 Champions League matches. He appeared in 115 international games for England and scored 17 times. He received an OBE in 2003, became a UNICEF Goodwill Ambassador in 2005, and was inducted into the English Football Hall of Fame in 2008.

Summary: David Beckham was one of the finest football players of his generation, and one of United's best players. He was one of the great free-kick takers in world football, scoring many goals using his trademark style. He is one of the most recognisable faces in the world and has become a global celebrity icon.

GEORGE BEST

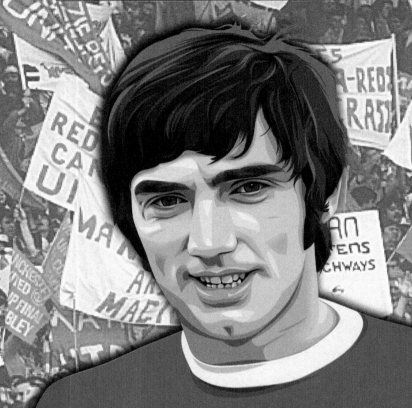

Born: 22nd May 1946
United Debut: 1963
Nationality: Northern Irish
Position: Winger/Midfielder
Height: 5 ft 9 in (1.75 m)
Major Trophies: 5

Early Career

George Best was born in the Northern Ireland capital, Belfast. He was playing for Cregagh boys club when, at the age of 15, Best was discovered by Manchester United scout Bob Bishop, whose telegram to United manager Matt Busby read: "I think I've found you a genius.". Best made his first team debut for United in a First Division fixture in September 1963, aged 17. He recorded his first goal in his second game three months later, after having played in the reserves. He captained the side that won the FA Youth Cup in 1964. He was given a job as an errand boy on the Manchester Ship Canal as English clubs were not allowed to give apprentice contracts to Northern Irish players.

Later Career

In the 1964/65 season, Best helped United to win the league title in his first full season. He made a name for himself when scoring two goals against Benfica in a European Cup quarter-final game in March 1966, aged just 19 after which the Portuguese press nicknamed him "El Beatle". He was instrumental in United winning the European Cup in 1968, scoring a solo goal in the final in extra time, having already scored the only goal in the semi-final first-leg win over Real Madrid, before assisting the winning goal in the second leg. He scored 28 goals that season in 41 league games, his career-best, and 32 in total. He won the Ballon d'Or for being the best player in Europe. He smashed six past Northampton Town in a 1970 FA Cup tie including a well-known 'feint' on the goalkeeper when going past for the sixth goal. He received an invitation from the then UK Prime Minister who was a fan. Best hit two hat-tricks and scored from a solo run where he beat four defenders during the 1971/72 season and finished as the club's top goalscorer in the league for the fifth consecutive season; he had 26 in all. He announced his retirement soon after, and appeared in his final game in January 1974, as United suffered the ignominy of relegation at the end of the season. He then played for several teams, having stints in the USA, Scotland, South Africa, Ireland, and Australia. During his international days with Northern Ireland, he was best remembered for once beating England goalkeeper Gordon Banks to a ball and scoring a goal. However, it was disallowed. He competed in his final career match in 1984 for Irish side Tobermore United. Best was honoured with a testimonial game four years later and scored twice. He suffered from alcoholism during his time at United and in his later career and life which led to disciplinary issues.

Accomplishments

Best scored 179 goals in 470 games for Manchester United over 11 seasons and 251 goals in 705 games throughout his career. With United, he won the First Division twice and the European Cup once. For Northern Ireland, he played 37 times and struck nine goals. He was a Hall of Fame inductee and received a PFA Merit Award.

Summary: George Best was one of the most naturally gifted and talented footballers in the history of football. He was skilful at dribbling with the ball and had celebrity status and a colourful lifestyle. He passed away in November 2005 due to complications caused by his alchol problems.

ERIC CANTONA

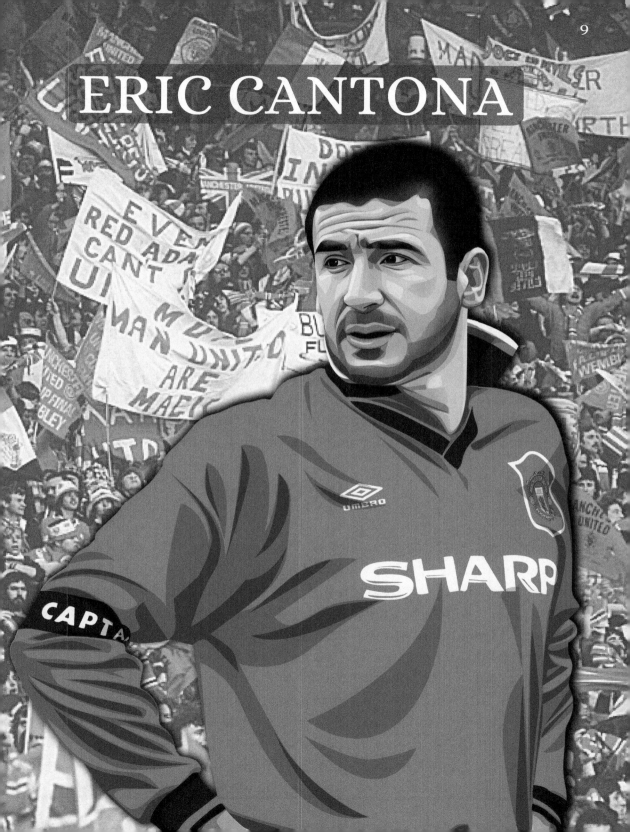

Born: 24th May 1966
United Debut: 1992
Nationality: French
Position: Forward
Height: 1.87 m (6 ft 2 in)
Trophies: 9

Early Career

Eric Daniel Pierre Cantona was born in the city of Marseille in France. The house he grew up in was part of a cave where previous generations of his family lived. He began his youth career with French team SO Les Caillols at the age of 14. He became a professional with AJ Auxerre in 1983 and scored his first goal for the club the following season. He joined boyhood team Marseille in 1988, before joining another French side, Nimes, in 1991. Despite some controversy over the years, Cantona signed for English First Division team Leeds United in January 1992 for £1m. He made his debut a month later.

Later Career

His first goal came three weeks after his debut. Despite playing only 15 games and scoring three goals, Cantona was still seen as a major member of the team that won the First Division title in his first season there. He recorded the first-ever hat-trick in the newly formed Premier League in August 1992. He made a controversial move to fierce rivals Manchester United in November 1992. United initially called Leeds about the availability of future club legend Denis Irwin and only after did they enquire about Cantona. With his presence, United lost just twice in the league as the club picked up its first championship in 26 years. Cantona was the first player to win consecutive English top division titles with different clubs and was his third consecutive title after winning one with Marseille two years previously. He converted two penalties in the FA Cup Final triumph and was the club's top scorer with 25 goals as the double was achieved in 1994. However, in January 1995 he was involved in a controversial incident on the field and banned for eight months. In his comeback game, he provided an assist and scored a goal. Cantona was the victorious captain in the 1996 FA Cup Final win, as well as scoring the only goal. He was the skipper for the following season as title number four in five years with the club was achieved, and six in seven in total for himself. One of his most memorable goals, a magnificent chip against Sunderland, was followed by an iconic celebration. He announced his retirement from the game at the early age of 30 at the end of the 1996/97 season. His final match was a testimonial game for another player in May. He had become an iconic figure at Old Trafford amongst the fans and was honoured with a testimonial in 1998. He was involved with the French team in beach soccer and won the World title in 2005. After retiring, he became an actor in French cinema.

Accomplishments

Cantona made 185 appearances for United, netting 82 times. He won the League four times, and the FA Cup twice with United, as well as the First Division with Leeds United, and the French Division 1 twice with Marseille. For the French national team, he played 45 times scoring 20 goals. He was inducted into both the English Football and Premier League Halls of Fame.

Summary: Eric Cantona was quite simply one of the most talented players of his generation but also one of the most controversial. He is known for his upturned collar and swagger on and off the pitch.

BOBBY CHARLTON

Born: 11th October 1937
United Debut: 1956
Nationality: English
Position: Midfielder/Forward
Height: 5 ft 7 in (1.70 m)
Major Trophies: 9

Early Career

Robert Charlton was born in the town of Ashington, Northumberland. He is related to many well-known professional footballers including Newcastle legend Jackie Milburn. Whilst playing for his school, Charlton was scouted by United aged just 15, in 1953. He undertook an electrical engineering apprenticeship before turning professional a year later. He was a regular scorer in both the youth and reserve teams, and he eventually made his senior debut in October 1956 scoring two goals.

Later Career

He scored his first hat-trick four months later as United went on to win the title. Having survived the Munich air disaster tragedy in February 1958, Charlton was handed his first England international cap against Scotland two months later. He was the club's top scorer with 29 league goals in 38 games during the 1958/59 season as United came second in the table. He won his first FA Cup winners' medal in 1963 at his third attempt. He had scored two goals in the quarter-final victory. His best performance in a European competition came in 1964/65 as the club took part in the Inter-Cities Fairs Cup. He notched eight goals in 11 matches, including a hat-trick. Charlton represented England in the 1966 World Cup tournament and netted three goals during the competition. He played in the final as the nation won its first-ever major international tournament, beating West Germany in the final and was voted European Footballer of the Year. Charlton struck twice in the final as United lifted their first European Cup in 1968. Playing as the captain, he scored with a header in the second half as the match finished level at full-time, before scoring in the 99th minute as the club became the first English side to triumph in the competition. The club had also won the First Division title twice in three years with the success in 1967 being Charlton's final league honour. His final appearance for his club came in April 1973, He then became player-manager of Preston North End for two seasons before becoming a member of Manchester United's board of directors in 1984.

Accomplishments

He netted 249 goals in 758 matches for the team, both club records at the time. He won the league three times, the European Cup once, and the FA Cup once. He played 106 international games with England and scored a record 49 goals (both records at the time). He was a member of the 1966 World Cup-winning team and received the Ballon d'Or award in 1966. Charlton was honoured with the OBE in 1969, the CBE in 1974, and became a Knight Bachelor (knighted), in 1994. He was an English Football Hall of Fame inductee in 2002.

Summary: Bobby Charlton is considered one of the greatest players of all time and is arguably Manchester United's greatest of all time. He had an outstanding goal scoring record from midfield and broke many appearance and goal scoring records for both club and country.

DUNCAN EDWARDS

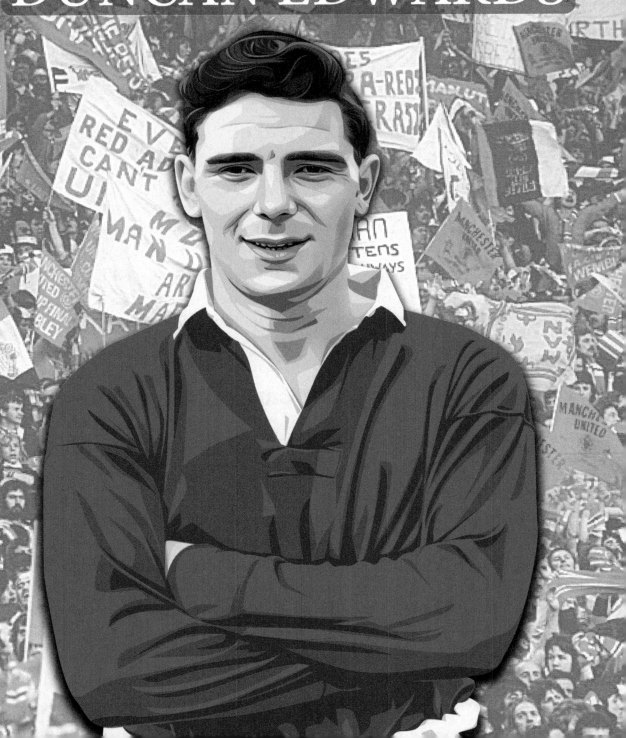

Born: 1st October 1936
United Debut: 1953
Nationality: English
Position: Midfielder
Height: 5 ft 11 in (1.80 m)
Major Trophies: 4

Early Career

Born in Dudley, West Midlands, Duncan Edwards played football for his school and various local teams. He was selected to have a trial with the English Schools under-14 team at the Football Association. He made the cut and made his debut at Wembley Stadium in 1950, going on to captain the team for two seasons. He was scouted by Jack O'Brien who reported back to manager Matt Busby in 1948 that he had "today seen a 12-year-old schoolboy who merits special watching. His name is Duncan Edwards, of Dudley".

Later Career

Edwards played in the team that won the first-ever FA Youth Cup in 1953. He had already made his debut for the first team in April. At 16 years, he was the youngest player ever to play in the top division of English football. He was one of the young footballers referred to as the 'Busby Babes' a group of gifted and talented individuals trained and developed by the club's own youth team to eventually progress to senior level and gain the top honours. He made 24 league appearances during the 1953/54 season and won his second consecutive Youth Cup honour. The 1954/55 campaign saw Edwards as an established member of the team playing 36 times and scoring the first six goals of his career. When he made his international debut for the England national team in April 1955, Edwards broke another record by becoming the youngest player to play for the nation since the Second World War. He then spent two years in the British Army as part of the compulsory National Service scheme. He played football for the army during this time. After returning to the United team, he helped the club win the league title in 1956, competing in 33 games, before playing a game extra the following season as the club retained the First Division. He was part of the team that won 10-0 versus Anderlecht as United made their first appearance in the European Cup competition in 1956/57. He scored two goals for England against Denmark in a World Cup qualifying game in late 1956. Edwards began the 1957/58 season in good form and rumours abounded that top Italian clubs were seeking to sign him. Manchester United qualified for the semi-finals of the European Cup by beating Red Star Belgrade on aggregate in February 1958. The plane returning home from the match crashed on take-off in Munich, Germany. Edwards was severely injured and taken to hospital but was unable to recover and passed away. He was aged just 21.

Accomplishments

Edwards played in a total of 151 league games for United, scoring 20 times in six seasons. He won the First Division championship twice. For England, he played in 18 internationals scoring five goals. He was inducted into the inaugural English Football Hall of Fame in 2002.

Summary: Duncan Edwards was a player of immense strength and toughness. He was touted to achieve bigger things before tragedy struck. A versatile player who could play many positions, he was predominately a holding midfielder. Despite his age, many of his contemporaries have described him as one of, if not the best player with whom they had played.

RIO FERDINAND

Born: 7th November 1978
United Debut: 2002
Nationality: English
Position: Centre-back/defender
Height: 6 ft 2 in (1.89 m)
Major Trophies: 14

Early Career

Born in the South London district of Camberwell, Rio Gavin Ferdinand was a very talented sportsman, excelling at gymnastics and ballet as well as football whilst at school. He joined the youth squad of West Ham United in 1992, having already trained with various football clubs. He was given a debut by West Ham in May 1996 and played over 100 league games for the club. Ferdinand had made his debut for the England national team in November 1997 aged just 19, making him the youngest defender to represent the country. He then signed for Premier League side Leeds United in November 2000 as the world's most expensive defender at £18m, but less than two years later, he joined rivals Manchester United as the most expensive British footballer in 2002 for around £30m.

Later Career

Ferdinand made his debut for the club a month after joining and was triumphant in winning the Premier League in his first season there, after playing in 28 matches. It took him three years to score his first goal for the club in December 2005 and then grabbed a last-minute winner against Liverpool a month later. He was part of the defensive line-up that let in no goals for six consecutive matches at the start of the 2007/08 season. He struck his first European goal in October. Five months later, he was called upon to stand in as a goalkeeper during a FA Cup quarter-final tie against Portsmouth. In May, he captained the Manchester United team to victory in the Champions League Final against fellow Premier League side Chelsea, winning on penalties to help the club achieve the double that season. A third successive League title followed a season later. He missed much of the 2009/10 campaign due to injuries. Ferdinand scored the winner and final goal in manager Alex Ferguson's last game at Old Trafford, in May 2013, hitting the net with a volley from a corner. He left the club a year later, having played his last match a day before the announcement. He then signed for newly promoted side Queens Park Rangers, but after just a dozen appearances, he eventually retired from the field of play in May 2015. He became a football pundit on television and even tried his hand at boxing but was unable to attain a licence.

Accomplishments

Ferdinand played 312 league games for Manchester United and scored seven goals. He appeared in over 450 games for the club, including 91 times in Europe. His career league matches totalled 514 with 11 goals. He was victorious in the League six times, the Champions League once, and the League Cup twice with United. He played 81 times for England and scored three goals. He participated in ten World Cup finals matches and no goals were conceded in seven of those games. He was an English Football Hall of Fame inductee in 2016 and has an honorary degree from London South Bank University.

Summary: Rio Ferdinand was one of the best defenders of his generation and was a stalwart for 12 seasons at the club. He formed one of the Premier Leagues great centre-back partnerships with Serbian Nemanja Vidić. He is currently a television football pundit.

BILL FOULKES

Born: 5th January 1932
United Debut: 1951
Nationality: English
Position: Defender
Height: 5 ft 11 in (1.80 m)
Major Trophies: 9

Early Career

William Anthony Foulkes was born in the town of St Helens, Lancashire (now Merseyside). His father and grandfather were both rugby league players. He played for a boys club in his teens and worked as a miner. Whilst playing for his club, he was spotted by First Division team Manchester United and he was invited to play for the junior side in 1950. Over a year later he turned professional and made his senior debut against Liverpool in December 1952 aged 20. His maiden goal for the club came over a year later when he managed to find the back of the net from near the halfway line.

Later Career

He won his first league title with the team in the 1955/56 season and followed it up by helping the team successfully defend their title the following year. That same season he played in all eight games in Europe as United represented English football for the first time in the event. The team reached the semi-finals, and included the record-breaking ten-nil win over Anderlecht. Having survived the Munich air disaster in 1958, Foulkes became the team captain. He became one of the senior figures in the team and the club finished runners-up in the league in 1958/59. However, Foulkes and the team struggled in the following seasons due to the tragic events. He played in the majority of the matches, but the club finished a lowly 19th in the 1962/63 season. However, they caused a surprise by winning the FA Cup in May 1963, beating the more fancied Leicester City in the final. Foulkes played in all six games in the successful Cup run. Having finished second in the league the season before, United finally regained the championship in 1965. This was followed by another League title two years later, giving Foulkes his fourth winners' medal and making him the most successful club player of the era. United made another foray into Europe in 1967/68 and reached the semi-finals where they played Real Madrid. In the second leg, with the aggregate scores level, Foulkes latched onto a cross from George Best to send his team into the final. They triumphed in the final beating Benfica, giving Foulkes his first European Cup success at the age of 36. He played his final game for the club in August 1969 at the age of 37. His 688 competitive matches were a record for the club at the time, and with a career span of 18 seasons, he was the longest-serving player in the club's history when he retired. He stayed on as a youth team coach before taking on coaching for over 20 years, mainly overseas.

Accomplishments

Foulkes played in 566 league matches for United and a record 688 games in 18 seasons scoring nine goals. His successes included the League four times, the European Cup once, and the FA Cup once. He won a sole cap for England in 1955.

Summary: Bill Foulkes was one of Manchester United's longest-serving players. He was part of the famed 'Busby Babes' outfit during the '50s and '60s and is fourth on United's all-time appearance list. He has been described as an old-fashioned stopper who loved facing big, strong centre-forwards. He passed away in November 2013 aged 81.

RYAN GIGGS

Born: 29th November 1973
United Debut: 1990
Nationality: Welsh
Position: Midfielder
Height: 5 ft 10 in (1.79 m)
Major Trophies: 34

Early Career

Ryan Joseph Wilson was born in the small district of Canton, in Cardiff, Wales. His family moved to the city of Salford, England, in 1980, where Giggs competed for a local team. He was spotted and signed for Manchester City's school of excellence. He was then offered a trial at rivals Manchester United after scoring a hat-trick against their youth team as Sir Alex watched on. He took his mother's name 'Giggs' when he was 16 and became a professional in December 1990. He made his league debut against Everton in March 1991 and scored his first goal two months later in the Manchester derby.

Later Career

Giggs became a regular during the 1991/92 season, whilst also playing for the youth team. His first major trophy was the League Cup triumph in 1992, when he provided the assist for the only goal, having scored the winning goal in the semi-final. He was the club's first choice left-winger in the first season of the Premier League in 1992/93, and the 'double' of League and Cup triumphs followed a season later. He was the first player to win two consecutive Young Player of the Year awards. During the 1998/99 season, Giggs missed a lot of games due to injury, but his big contribution came as he netted his legendary extra-time goal in the FA Cup semi-final against Arsenal and then scored a 90th-minute equaliser against Juventus in the Champions

League semi. In the FA Cup Final, he set up the equalising goal, as the club achieved a treble. In 2002, he became the club's longest-serving player. After a trying period, he came up trumps with two goals in a Champions League game in 2003, including a wonder goal, in one of his best games. When Manchester United won the Premier League title in 2007, Giggs set a new English record of nine league titles under his name. In May 2008, he made his 759th appearance for the club, a new record, and converted the winning penalty in the Champions League Final. He then became the record league appearance holder for the club with 607 in 2011. Giggs had scored in 23 consecutive seasons in the league by 2013 and made his 1000th professional appearance in the same year. Later in the year, he became the all-time record holder for appearances made in Champions League competition. He retired in May 2014 at the age of 40 and went into management.

Accomplishments

Playing his entire career at Manchester United, Giggs played an astonishing 963 games and scored 168 goals including a record 157 Champions League appearances. He won a record 13 Premier league titles, as well as two Champions Leagues and four FA Cup triumphs. At the time, he had made the most individual appearances in the Premier League. For the Wales national team, he won 64 caps and scored 12 goals. He received an OBE in 2007 and was inducted into the English Football Hall of Fame in 2005.

Summary: Ryan Giggs was a speedy left-winger and United's longest-serving player ever who holds many club records. He had a spell as United's interim and assistant manager and now manages Wales.

MARK HUGHES

Born: 1st November 1963
United Debut: 1980
Nationality: Welsh
Position: Striker/Midfielder
Height: 5 ft 11 in (1.80 m)
Major Trophies: 11

Early Career

Born in the small village of Ruabon, Wales, Leslie Mark Hughes joined United in 1980 after leaving school and being spotted by a scout. He made his first team debut three years later, scoring in a League Cup tie against Oxford United. He scored 24 goals in 55 games in the 1984/85 season, as the club was victorious in the FA Cup. On his international debut for Wales in 1984, Hughes scored the winning goal in just 17 minutes playing against England. He recorded a career-best 17 league strikes during the 1985/86 season, before embarking on a stint with Spanish side Barcelona in 1986 for a fee of £2m.

Later Career

He stayed just one season in Spain before being loaned to German side Bayern Munich where he famously played two matches in one day, first for Wales in Prague before flying back to Germany to play for Bayern later that day. Hughes returned to United in May 1988 for a club-record fee of £1.8 million. He became the first player from the club to win the PFA Player of the Year accolade in 16 years when he was the joint top goalscorer during the 1988/89 season. He struck two goals in the amazing 1990 FA Cup Final versus Crystal Palace as the game ended 3-3. United won the replay to collect their first trophy in five years. Hughes netted another couple of important goals playing Barcelona as Manchester United won the UEFA Cup Winners' Cup in the 1991 final. The last of his four hat-tricks for the club came in the 1990/91 season. In May 1993, he finally picked up a league winners' medal, when the club won the inaugural Premier League. He was the top scorer in the campaign with 15 goals. The following season, Hughes achieved the league and cup double with United, scoring in both the FA and League Cup Finals. In the semi-final of the former competition, he had struck a spectacular equaliser in the final minutes of extra time. He scored another 22 goals during the season. He managed two quick goals during United's record-breaking 9-0 victory over Ipswich Town in 1995, and eventually played his last game for the club in the 1995 FA Cup Final. Hughes then had playing spells with Chelsea, Southampton, and Everton, before playing his final career game with Blackburn Rovers in 2002. Hughes made over 100 Premier League appearances whilst also being the manager of Wales. He has since managed six Premier League clubs, Blackburn, Man City, Fulham, QPR, Stoke City and Southampton before taking charge of League 2 Bradford City in 2022 after a four-year break from the game.

Accomplishments

In two spells with Manchester United, Hughes scored 163 goals in 473 games and 224 goals in 799 club games in his career. The major honours included the Premier League twice, the FA Cup three times, and the Cup Winners' Cup once with United, together with the FA Cup once and the Cup Winners' Cup once with Chelsea. For Wales, he played in 72 internationals and scored 16 times. He was honoured with an OBE and a Hall of Fame induction.

Summary: Mark Hughes, nicknamed 'Sparky' was one of Manchester United's most reliable and hard-working footballers and described by Sir Alex as the best big-game player he has ever known. He went into football management after retiring.

DENIS IRWIN

Born: 31st October 1965
United Debut: 1990
Nationality: Irish
Position: Left-back
Height: 5 ft 8 in (1.73 m)
Major Trophies: 18

Early Career

Joseph Denis Irwin was born in the city of Cork in Ireland, and played Gaelic football and hurling at school. His youth career began at Second Division side Leeds United, and he played his first professional game for the club in 1983. Three years later, he moved to Oldham Athletic and played over 150 league matches for the club. He helped the team reach the semi-final of the FA Cup and the final of the League Cup in the 1989/90 season. In 1990, he was signed by Manchester United for £625,000 and he made his debut against Liverpool two months later.

Later Career

In his first season with the club, he was a member of the team that won the European Cup Winners' Cup playing in the final against Barcelona. He played in 34 league games and 52 matches during that season. Irwin then helped United to win the inaugural Premier League in 1992/93, starring in 40 of the 42 league games that season. He continued to represent the team in the majority of the games with a total of 62 as the club achieved the League and Cup double in 1993/94. He scored a goal in the semi-final replay victory as the side reached the final. Irwin upped his goal tally to six the following season, including four in the FA Cup run as he bagged two in a Fourth Round game before striking one in the semi-final against former club Oldham. He helped United to become the first English side to achieve the League and Cup double twice in 1995/96. The most memorable season was the 1998/99 year when the club achieved an unprecedented treble. He played 29 times in the league, with six FA Cup appearances and 12 in Europe, taking part in the dramatic final versus Bayern Munich. He aided the team to two more successive League championships, and was honoured with a testimonial game in August 2000. Irwin competed in his final season in 2001/02, and played in his final game in May, being made the team captain for the day. It has been said by United's most successful manager Alex Ferguson that Irwin was probably the finest signing he had ever made. Even in his mid-thirties, he was still United's first-choice left-back in preference to the much younger Phil Neville. He then joined Wolverhampton Wanderers where he played alongside ex-United teammate Paul Ince, winning promotion to the Premier League in his first season. He was applauded by the Old Trafford crowd on his return to the stadium with Wolves.

Accomplishments

Irwin played 529 matches for United and netted 33 goals in 12 seasons. He played exactly 900 club games in his whole career. With United, he won the Premier League seven times, the Champions League once, the Cup Winners' Cup once, and the FA Cup twice. For the Republic of Ireland he played 56 times and scored four goals including appearances at the 1994 World Cup. He was inducted into the Hall of Fame in 2016.

Summary: Denis Irwin was one of Manchester United's most solid and reliable defenders. With 18 trophies he is the joint-most successful Irish football player in history and is one of the club's greatest bargains.

ROY KEANE

Born: 10th August 1971
United Debut: 1993
Nationality: Irish
Position: Midfielder
Height: 5 ft 10 in (1.78 m)
Major Trophies: 17

Early Career

Born in the city of Cork, in Ireland, Roy Maurice Keane played football and took up boxing in his youth. He worked in temporary jobs while trying to develop as a footballer, and eventually signed for local team Cobh Ramblers in 1989. Keane was spotted by Nottingham Forest and he joined them in 1990 for £47,000 playing under Brian Clough. He made his first team debut in August against Liverpool and scored his first goal versus Sheffield United four months later. In 1993, Forest were relegated, and Keane made a move to United for a British record fee after a move to Blackburn Rovers collapsed at the last minute.

Later Career

His home debut in August 1993 saw Keane net two goals before securing the winner in a 3-2 comeback win over Manchester City. By the end of the season, he had captured both the League and Cup titles with the team. He was selected as the club captain for the 1997/98 season but missed most of the campaign through injury. When returning the following season, he led the side to a treble of big trophies, the domestic and Champions League, and the FA Cup. He scored the first goal as United came from 2-0 down to win 3-2 against Juventus in the Champions League semi-final. It was ranked as one of his best performances. However, he missed the final due to suspension, as United beat Bayern Munich. Keane helped United to win three successive league titles and won two Footballer/Player of the Year awards in 2000. In 2002/03 he led United to their third title in four years and his final major trophy with the club was the FA Cup triumph in 2003/04. He got his 50th goal for the club in 2005, whilst the FA Cup in the same season saw him make his seventh appearance in the final, a record at the time. After being injured early in the 2005/06 season, he decided to leave the club in November. His final game had been in September in a goal-less draw versus Liverpool. Keane was honoured with a testimonial game in May 2006 against Celtic. The crowd of over 69,000 was the largest for a testimonial in England. With nine major honours, he was the club's most successful captain. He played for Scottish side Celtic for one season, before managing various teams after his retirement.

Accomplishments

Keane made 480 appearances for United during his 13 seasons with the club scoring 51 times and was club captain for eight years. With United, he won the Premier League seven times, the Champions League once, and the FA Cup four times as well as a league title with Celtic. For the Republic of Ireland national team, he played 67 times and scored nine goals. He was inducted into both the English Football and Premier League Halls of Fame.

Summary: Roy Keane was a dominating box-to-box midfielder, noted for his aggressive and highly competitive style of play, an attitude that helped him excel as captain. He is now a popular pundit on tv.

DENIS LAW

Born: 24th February 1940
United Debut: 1962
Nationality: Scottish
Position: Forward
Height: 5 ft 9 in (1.75 m)
Major Trophies: 6

Early Career

Born in the village of Bucksburn, Aberdeen, in Scotland, Denis Law was born into a poor family. He showed a keen interest in football and was selected for the Scotland schoolboys team. He got his first opportunity with Huddersfield Town in 1954 as a 14-year-old after being spotted, and he was signed up a year later. He made his debut in December 1956 aged just 16, playing in a Second Division match. His former manager Bill Shankly wanted to take him to Liverpool four years later but he moved to Manchester City for a British record £55,000 fee, scoring on his debut. Another move then saw Law go abroad and join up with Italian side Torino in 1961, for a British record £110,000. He finally made his way to United in 1962, for yet another record fee of £115,000.

Later Career

Law scored after only seven minutes on his debut in August. He grabbed four goals in one game and also scored a couple of hat-tricks before netting the first goal in the FA Cup Final win against Leicester. He competed for a Rest of the World side against England during the 1963/64 season and ended the campaign with 46 goals in 42 games, still a club record, including 30 in 30 matches in the league. The following season he became the first and only Scottish footballer to win the Ballon d'Or award - for the best player in Europe – and helped his club to win the league title with another top-scoring 28 league goals. United regained the title in 1967, with Law again to the fore with 23 goals in the league. He missed out on playing in the triumphant 1968 European Cup Final due to injury. The following season, United reached the semi-finals of the competition, with Law having scored seven goals in two games in the First Round win over Waterford United. He was the top scorer in the tournament with nine goals. He continued to play for the club despite injury problems, before eventually playing his final game in 1973. He had recorded a total of 237 goals, putting him in second place in the club's all-time top goal scorers list. He moved back to Manchester City and played for one more season. In his final ever league game Law scored an 81st-minute backheel at Old Trafford to relegate United. He did not celebrate out of respect and the game was eventually abandoned due to pitch invasions but the 1-0 result stood.

Accomplishments

Law accumulated 171 league goals in 309 matches for Manchester United, and had a total of 237 in 404 games for the club in 11 years. He ended with over 300 goals in his entire career. There were two First Division titles, one European Cup, and one FA Cup, whilst with the team. For the Scottish national team, he scored a joint-record 30 goals in 55 international matches. He was honoured with a CBE in 2016, and was inducted into both the English and Scottish Football Halls of Fame.

Summary: Denis Law was one of Scotland's and Manchester United's best ever strikers. He had a statue erected outside the Old Trafford football ground depicting him in a line-up with other club legends, George Best and Bobby Charlton, named the 'Holy Trinity'.

GARY NEVILLE

Born: 18th February 1975
United Debut: 1992
Nationality: English
Position: Right-back
Height: 5 ft 11 in (1.80 m)
Major Trophies: 20

Early Career

Gary Alexander Neville was born in the town of Bury, Greater Manchester and joined United as an apprentice in 1991 after leaving school. In his first season, he won the FA Youth Cup as captain of the team. His first team debut came in a UEFA Cup game in September 1992 against Torpedo Moscow. He was part of a youth set-up that included future stars such as David Beckham, Ryan Giggs, Paul Scholes, and his younger brother Phil. He helped the club to achieve the league and cup double in 1995/96. He had made his first appearance for the England national team in June 1995. The first of only seven goals in his entire career with the club came in May 1997 against Middlesbrough.

Later Career

Once in his regular right-back defensive position, Neville stayed there during the following years and was part of the famous treble-winning team in 1999. Two more successive championships followed. The 2003/04 season saw Neville score two goals, his best scoring year, and the seventh and final goal of his career came in a Champions League game in November 2004, Sir Alex Ferguson's 1000th game with the club. He was given the captaincy in late 2005 and won his first trophy as skipper in the 2006 League Cup Final. After an injury, he made his comeback in a Champions League quarter-final tie, his 99th appearance in the competition. He stepped down as the team captain in 2010 due to making fewer appearances but managed to play his 600th game for the club in October. Neville played his final match on New Year's Day of 2011 against West Brom. He was honoured with a testimonial four months later in a game against Juventus. With his brother Phil, who also played as a defender, the pair played together at United for over ten years, winning ten major trophies together, including six League titles. His final trophy was the 2009/10 League Cup. He was a true one-club man having spent his entire 19-year career with the club. When he gave up playing, he was the second longest-serving footballer at the club. After retiring, Neville became England assistant manager and then took up football punditry on television after a short spell as manager of Valencia.

Accomplishments

Neville played a total of 400 league games for Manchester United scoring five goals. He appeared in 117 Champions League games, netting two goals, and had a career record of just over 600 games. He was captain for over five years. For England, he won 85 caps and played at five major tournaments. At United, he won eight Premier League titles, two Champions Leagues, three FA Cups, and two League Cups. He was an English Football Hall of Fame inductee in 2015, and he also received two honorary degrees.

Summary: Gary Neville is considered to be the best right-back in Premier League history and was best known for his work rate, professionalism, determination, and consistency as a defender as well as his loyalty to Manchester United.

GARY PALLISTER

Born: 30th June 1965
United Debut: 1989
Nationality: English
Position: Defender
Height: 6 ft 4 in (1.93 m)
Major Trophies: 15

Early Career

Gary Andrew Pallister was born in the seaside town of Ramsgate, Kent, but he grew up in County Durham where he supported nearby team Middlesbrough. He joined the club when aged 19, having started his career in the non-league. He spent five years there, helping the team to two consecutive promotions to the First Division in 1988. He made his England debut in 1988 whilst still playing in the Second Division. He was then signed by Manchester United in August 1989 for a fee of £2.3m, a record for a British defender at the time.

Later Career

He played his first senior game for United a day after joining the club and scored his first goal in November. Pallister gained his first success in the 1990 FA Cup and then the Cup Winners' Cup in 1991, forming a formidable defensive partnership with Steve Bruce as the club won the inaugural Premier League. He scored with a memorable free-kick in the final home game of the season against Blackburn Rovers. Pallister played all 42 league games in the title run. He netted the equaliser in extra time against Crystal Palace in the 1995 FA Cup semi-final to force a replay and scored again as United won. Both goals were scored with headers. Pallister became the major figure in defence after Bruce left for Birmingham City in 1996, but the club continued to prosper as a fourth league title in five years was collected in 1997. In his later career, he formed partnerships with David May and Ronny Johnsen. He netted two first half goals as United recorded an away win against Liverpool to virtually ensure the title for the club with a 3-1 win. He played his final game for United in 1998. Apart from the numerous titles, Pallister was involved with the team that came second or runners-up in six major competitions, including three times in the League. In nine years with the club, he was the only player to collect all the winners' honours under the management of Alex Ferguson and was also one of the club's longest-serving players. Aged 33, he moved back to Middlesbrough in the summer of 1998 for £2.5 million under the management of former teammate Bryan Robson. He played for three years before retiring in 2001 at the age of 36 having suffered from various injuries in the preceding seasons. He became a football pundit on television after retiring.

Accomplishments

Pallister won the Premier League four times, the FA Cup three times, the European Cup Winners' Cup once, and the League Cup once, with Manchester United. He was included in the First Division/Premier League Team of the Year five times in his nine years at the club. He made over 500 league appearances in his 17-year career. He won 22 caps for England but never appeared in a major tournament.

Summary: Gary Pallister was a pacy defender with excellent aerial ability and terrific ball control given his imposing 6ft 4in frame. He formed half of the "Dolly and Daisy" partnership with Steve Bruce, one of the best in United's history.

BRYAN ROBSON

Born: 11th January 1957
United Debut: 1981
Nationality: English
Position: Midfielder
Height: 5 ft 10 in (1.78 m)
Major Trophies: 9

Early Career

Bryan Robson was born in the town of Chester-le-Street, County Durham. He joined the cub scouts to get a chance at playing football on their team. Robson competed in athletics and football whilst at school, and he captained both the school football and district teams. He was signed up as an apprentice by West Bromwich Albion in 1972, having had trials with a few clubs. He made his first team debut in 1975 and scored his first goal in the next game, having played for the reserves for three years. He helped the club to a third-placed finish in the 1978/79 First Division season, before signing with fellow First Division club Manchester United in October 1981 for a British record fee of £1.5m.

Later Career

Robson made his debut six days later. His first goal came a month later. In the 1982 World Cup, he scored one of the fastest goals in its history for England against France after only 27 seconds. He netted a goal as United beat Arsenal in the semi-final of the 1983 FA Cup, and then scored twice in the final replay to clinch his first trophy as team captain. The club reached the semis of the Cup Winners' Cup the following season, with Robson striking another two goals in the quarter-final victory. He was the captain again as United were victorious in their second FA Cup success in three years. The next success again came, in the FA Cup in 1990. He scored the club's opening goal in the pulsating 3-3 draw in the final against Crystal Palace, and by winning in the replay, Robson became the first captain of the club to lift the FA Cup three times. He was honoured with a testimonial game in November 1990, and despite regular injury problems, continued to play and captain the side. He played long enough to be part of the inaugural Premier League triumph in 1992/93 - his first league title after 15 years – scoring his one and only goal of the season on the final day. He won another league winners' medal the following season and he competed in his first European Cup campaign at the age of 36. He left to become player-manager of Middlesbrough in 1994 where he remained for three seasons before retiring just before his 40th birthday. He then went on to manage several teams after his retirement including former club West Brom.

Accomplishments

Robson scored 99 goals in 461 matches for Manchester United, including 74 in 345 games in the league. He won two Premier League titles, four FA Cups, one League Cup, and one European Cup Winners' Cup. He won 90 caps for England, scoring 26 times. He captained the side in 64 matches, only two men have done so more times. He was awarded the OBE in 1990 and inducted into the English Football Hall of Fame in 2002.

Summary: Bryan Robson is remembered as an inspiring leader for both club and country. He was the longest-serving captain of the Old Trafford club and had a great goalscoring record from midfield.

CRISTIANO RONALDO

Born: 5th February 1985
United Debut: 2003
Nationality: Portuguese
Position: Forward
Height: 1.87 m (6 ft 2 in)
Major Trophies: 9

Early Career

Born on the island of Madeira, Portugal, Cristiano Ronaldo dos Santos Aveiro was born into a poor family. He competed for a local side from the age of seven and then left the island to join the academy of Sporting Lisbon. At the age of 15, he required surgery due to a heart problem. Two years later, in 2002, he made his first-team debut and scored his first two goals a few days later. His play attracted the attention of major clubs, and he was duly snapped up by United immediately after terrorising the red devils in a 2003 friendly match for a fee of £12.24m. He made his league debut a few days later against Bolton and then got his first goal in November against Portsmouth.

Later Career

The first Premier League honour came along in 2007 and he scored his first hat-trick for the club in early 2008. That season he notched a club record 42 goals. He went on to score his 100th goal for United, subsequently going on to win both the Ballon d'Or and the FIFA World Player of the Year at the end of 2008. He was then sold to Real Madrid for a world record £80m fee in August 2010. Ronaldo scored on his La Liga debut. Two four-goal hauls and four hat-tricks meant he became the first player to score 40 goals in a league season in 2010/11. A personal best 60 goals was attained in 2011/12, recording seven hat-tricks during the league campaign. With 100 league goals in 92 matches, he broke the club record. Records continued to fall as he pocketed 61 goals, and the fastest 200 La Liga goals in 178 matches, during the 2014/15 season. Five goals in one game, a club record 31 hat-tricks, and then becoming the club's all-time top goal scorer followed. His final game for the club came in 2018. He moved to Italian giants Juventus in 2018 for €100m where he won a Serie A title, before moving back to United in 2021 for £12.85m. His second debut for the club saw him score two goals, before breaking the record for the most appearances in Champions League games and then moving past the 800 career goal mark. He scored a hat-trick against Spurs and Norwich in his return season. According to various statistical records, he lays claim to being the greatest goal scorer in professional football history. He left the club in 2022 to join Al Nassr.

Accomplishments

In his first spell with United, Ronaldo scored 118 goals in 292 games, before recording an extraordinary 450 goals in 438 matches for Real Madrid. He netted 81 times in 98 league games for Juventus. The honours include three Premier Leagues, one Champions League, and one FA Cup with United; two La Ligas, and four Champions Leagues with Real; and two Serie A titles with Juventus. He has played over 1100 games and scored over 800 goals. For his national team Portugal, Ronaldo has appeared in a record 186 games and scored an all-time record of 115 international goals so far. He has triumphed in the European Championship once, and the Nations League once. Ronaldo has numerous records to his name in a career still ongoing. He has won the Ballon d'Or five times, second only to his great rival, Lionel Messi.

Summary: Cristiano Ronaldo is unquestionably one of the greatest footballers of all time. Known for his extraordinary work ethic and dedication, he is also known as a big-game player and a serial winner of trophies. He holds numerous all-time records for the sport and is the greatest goal scorer in international football history.

WAYNE ROONEY

Born: 24th October 1985
United Debut: 2004
Nationality: English
Position: Forward/Midfielder
Height: 5 ft 9 in (1.76 m)
Major Trophies: 16

Early Career

Born in the city of Liverpool, Wayne Mark Rooney played for a local schoolboys team and scored a record 72 goals in one season. He went on to attain 99 goals in a junior league season at the age of nine, and then 114 for the youth team soon after joining his boyhood team Everton. He made his debut for the club in August 2002, before becoming the club's youngest goal scorer two months later at the age of 16 with a stunning strike against Arsenal. In August 2004, Rooney was signed by Manchester United for around £27m, a record for a teenager. He made an instant impression by scoring a hat-trick on his debut in a Champions League game against Fenerbahçe. Having already been the youngest to score in a Premier League game, he now became the youngest to achieve the feat in the competition at 18.

Later Career

Rooney's first success with United came when he slotted in two goals in the 2006 League Cup Final. He won the Premier and Champions League double in 2007/08 scoring 18 goals. In 2008, he became the youngest player to appear in the Premier League 200 times. He scored four goals in a game in 2010 and was soon followed by goal number 100 in the Premier League. The 2009/10 season saw Rooney have one of his best scoring terms with 34 goals in 44 games, including 26 in 32 in the league. In early 2011, he produced one of the best goals of his career with an overhead bicycle kick versus Manchester City. A succession of hat-tricks put him on seven for the club in 2011. In 2012, he played in his 500th career game and marked it by putting two past Liverpool. He had the best assist record for the domestic and Champions league combined with 18 in the 2013/14 campaign. He was named captain for the 2014/15 season, and later in the year won his 100th cap for England, scoring his 44th international goal. Many records followed; most goals for one Premier League side (since broken), 100 league assists, most goals in Europe by a club player, and then the most goals for the club in history. Later in his United career, he dropped into a deeper playmaking role. Rooney's final game for United came in the 2017 Europa League Final against Ajax, coming on as a substitute as the team won the title. He returned to Everton in 2017 and then had brief stints in the USA and at Derby County. Rooney played his final career game in 2020/ 2021 before taking the manager's role at the Midlands club. He had ended his England career in 2018 as the nation's record goal scorer.

Accomplishments

Rooney appeared in 559 games for Manchester United and scored a record 253 goals. There were 183 goals in 393 league matches. His honours with the club included five league titles, one Champions League, one FA Cup, and one Europa League. He played 120 times for England and scored a record 53 goals, playing at six major tournaments. He was recently inducted into the Premier League Hall of Fame in 2022.

Summary: Wayne Rooney is Manchester United's all-time leading scorer and the only player to have scored 250 goals for the Reds. He was known for his tireless work rate, competitive drive and sensational finishing.

JACK ROWLEY

Born: 7th October 1918
United Debut: 1937
Nationality: English
Position: Forward
Height: 5 ft 9 in (1.75 m)
Major Trophies: 3

Early Career

John Frederick Rowley was born in the city of Wolverhampton, West Midlands and began his career with local team Wolverhampton Wanderers in 1935 but failed to make a first-team appearance. He then played in the non-league before catching the attention of Second Division side Manchester United, who signed him in 1937 for £3,000.

Later Career

Aged just 17, Rowley made his debut for the team and struck four goals in his second professional game against Swansea City, just over a month later, in a 5-1 win. United were promoted back to the First Division in his first season there. Initially bought as an outside left, he was to develop into a highly effective centre-forward in Matt Busby's first United team. As competitive league football was suspended with the outbreak of war, Rowley served in the South Staffordshire Regiment, participating in the D-Day landings at Normandy in 1945. After the war, Rowley helped the team to claim the FA Cup trophy in 1948, scoring two goals in the final versus Blackpool. He had recorded five goals in the competition in six games. It was the club's first major trophy in 37 years. Having notched a career-best 26 goals in the league when United came second in 1946/47, Rowley's sustained high goal scoring came to fruition in 1951/52 when he guided the team to their first League title in 41 years, with another personal best performance of 30 league goals in 40 matches scoring four hat-tricks along the way. Previously, he had put five past Yeovil Town in a FA Cup tie in 1949. In 1947, he had twice scored four goals in a match. His last game was in January 1954 in a FA Cup tie, having scored his last goal two weeks earlier. He was one of the original players who played under the management of Matt Busby. When he left the club in 1955 he had become the first player to score over 200 goals for the club. He moved to Plymouth Argyle to become their player-manager where he spent five years in total and managed a few teams after retiring including Ajax, having played his final game in 1957. His brother Arthur still holds the record for the most goals scored ever in the history of the English Football League with 434. He ran a post office/newsagent in Oldham after leaving football.

Accomplishments

Rowley spent 12 seasons at Manchester United, and in that time scored 211 goals in 424 matches, a record at the time. In the league, he recorded 182 goals in 380 games. Five times he got over 20 goals in a season. In his career, he bagged 238 goals in 504 matches. His honours included one First Division title and one FA Cup success both with United. He played six internationals for the England national team and netted six goals, including four in one game against Northern Ireland in 1949.

Summary: Jack Rowley was one of Manchester United's most prolific goal scorers and was a key member of United's post-war success. He held the club goal scoring record for a number of years and was nicknamed 'The Gunner' due to his shooting abilities. He passed away in June 1998.

PETER SCHMEICHEL

Born: 18th November 1963
United Debut: 1991
Nationality: Danish
Position: Goalkeeper
Height: 6 ft 3 in (1.91 m)
Major Trophies: 15

Early Career

Peter Boleslaw Schmeichel was born in the town of Gladsaxe, in Denmark, and started his football career playing for a local team near the town of Buddinge. He played his first game at the age of eight and continued playing youth team football before being promoted to senior duties for Gladsaxe-Hero in 1981. He moved to another Danish team Hvidovre, before being picked up by one of the top clubs in the league, Brondby IF. From 1987 to 1991, Schmeichel won the league four times in five years with the club making 139 appearances.

Later Career

Schmeichel was signed in August 1991 by United for £505,000, a price later described by Sir Alex as "the bargain of the century". In his first season, United were runners-up in the league, but he gained success with his country Denmark, as they surprisingly won the 1992 European Championship, putting in some fine performances. In the inaugural season of the Premier League, Schmeichel did not concede a goal in 22 games as United won their first League title in 26 years. The following season, the club achieved the League and Cup double. Two more consecutive League triumphs followed in 1996 and 1997. In his final season with the club, United won an unprecedented treble. He saved a vital penalty against Arsenal in the semi-final of the FA

Cup, as United went on to win in extra time. In the Premier League, he played 34 of the 38 games, as the club lost just five times during the whole season in all competitions, including just three in the league. He competed in all 13 Champions League matches, conceding just five goals in the final five rounds against the likes of Inter Milan, Juventus, and Bayern Munich. In the absence of Roy Keane, he was selected as captain for the Final. In an unforgettable celebratory moment, Schmeichel was shown cartwheeling gleefully in his area after Solskjær's winning goal. He kept clean sheets in a staggering 42% of games he played for the club. He scored one goal for the club in a UEFA Cup game in 1995. After United, Schmeichel played for Sporting Lisbon, before having short spells with Aston Villa and Manchester City. He retired after one season at City at the age of 39.

Accomplishments

In eight seasons with United, Schmeichel played in 398 games and made 748 club appearances overall for six different clubs scoring 11 goals. His main trophies included the Danish First Division four times with Brøndby, the Premier League five times, the Champions League once, the FA Cup three times with United, and also a league title with Sporting CP. For Denmark, he represented the team a record 129 times in 14 years. He grabbed one goal and won the European Championship once. He was honoured with the MBE in 2001, and inducted into both the English and Danish Football Halls of Fame.

Summary: Peter Schmeichel is regarded as one of the greatest goalkeepers of all-time. He had an immense presence in goal due to his size and was a fierce competitor.

PAUL SCHOLES

Born: 16th November 1974
United Debut: 1993
Nationality: English
Position: Midfielder
Height: 5 ft 6 in (1.68 m)
Major Trophies: 25

Early Career

Born in the city of Salford, Greater Manchester, Scholes excelled at both football and cricket whilst at school. He became part of the Manchester United team at the age of 14, eventually playing for the youth team. He turned professional in 1993 and scored two goals on his debut in September 1994 in a League Cup tie. He then scored on his Premier League debut three days later. He was one of the top goal scorers when Manchester United again achieved the League and Cup double in 1995/96, becoming the first English club to do it twice.

Later Career

Scholes struck a goal in the 1999 FA Cup Final as the club achieved a unique treble in 1998/99, playing a major part in all three competition wins. In March 2000, his volley against Bradford City was rated as one of the goals of the season, and he recorded his maiden hat-trick for the club a week later. With 20 goals during the 2002/03 campaign, Scholes had one of his best scoring seasons, and he won his third and final FA Cup medal the following season, scoring the winning goal in the semi-final against Arsenal. He played his 500th match for the club in 2006. Two years later, he played in his 100th Champions League game against Barcelona, a game in which he scored a stunning long-range effort - the only goal in the second leg tie which put United into the final which they won against Chelsea. It was match number 600 in 2009, as United won their third league title in succession that season.

When he scored his 25th goal in the Champions League in 2010, he became the highest-scoring central midfielder in the competition's history. He announced his retirement in May 2011 and was given a testimonial just over two months later. He joined the coaching staff at the club before injuries and a desire to play again saw him make a comeback to the team in January 2012. He played 21 times on his comeback and added a final league title, before finally hanging up his boots for good in May 2013. He scored in 19 consecutive Premier League seasons and was third on the list of appearances made for United. He was also the holder of the most Premier League titles by an English player. He briefly managed Oldham and Salford after retiring.

Accomplishments

Scholes played his entire 20-season career at Manchester United, recording 107 goals in 499 league games. He appeared in 718 matches in his career and scored a total of 155 goals. There were 134 appearances in European competition with 26 goals. The main successes included 11 Premier League titles, two Champions League titles, three FA Cups, and two League Cups. He played in 66 internationals for England and scored 14 goals but retired from international football in 2004 citing his family life and United career as more important. He was an English Football Hall of Fame inductee in 2008.

Summary: A misplaced Scholes pass was one of the rarest sights in football. His superb eye for goal and late runs from midfield made him a goalscoring threat during his career. He earned high praise from other legends of the game including Zidane and Xavi with Thierry Henry describing him as the Premier League's greatest ever player.

OLE GUNNAR SOLSKJÆR

Born: 26th February 1973
United Debut: 1996
Nationality: Norwegian
Position: Forward
Height: 5 ft 10 in (1.78 m)
Major Trophies: 12

Early Career

Ole Gunnar Solskjaer was born in the town of Kristiansund in Norway. He joined up with the local team Clausenengen at the age of seven. Ten years later, he made his first team debut for the club, and helped them gain promotion to the Third Division of the Norwegian league in 1993. He scored 31 out of the 48 club goals in his final season with the team. After five years, Solskjaer left the club with an impressive 115 goals in 109 matches. He then joined Tippeligaen club Molde FK and produced another 41 goals in 54 matches with the club.

Later Career

When he was signed by United in 1996, he was a relatively unknown player. It was expected that he'd be back up to Eric Cantona and Andy Cole. However, he netted after only six minutes in his debut game as a substitute in August and made 33 league appearances as United won the title. He was the club's top goalscorer in the league with 18 goals in his inaugural season. Solskjær stayed at Old Trafford even though other clubs showed interest in the player in 1998. He refused an offer from Tottenham Hotspur after United had accepted a £5.5 million bid for him. He continued to notch up two goals in a game a few times in the following season and scored the winning goal in injury time against Liverpool in an FA Cup tie in early 1999. One of his finest performances came in a league game a few days later, when coming on as a substitute he put four past the hapless Nottingham Forest team in the final dozen minutes of the match in an 8-1 win. This remains a Premier League record for goals by a substitute. His finest moment came in the Champions League Final three months later, when again as a sub he came on with just under ten minutes to go and scored the winning goal in injury time to spark jubilant celebrations whilst securing the treble. He bagged four goals against Everton in late 1999, and with more goal scoring as a substitute, he helped United to win their third consecutive league title in 2001, Solskjaer's fourth with the club. His knack of scoring two goals in a game continued in 2001/02 with six during the season. He captained the team a few times in the season after. He also earnt the man of the match award in the semi-final against Arsenal as the club lifted the FA Cup in 2004. After injury setbacks, he decided to retire and played his final game in 2007 in the FA Cup Final. As a substitute, he scored a record 28 goals for Manchester United. Over 68,000 fans turned out at his testimonial match in August 2008.

Accomplishments

In 235 league games, Solskjaer scored 91 times for United, with a total of 237 in 386 league matches during his career. He won six Premier Leagues, one Champions League, and two FA Cups in his 11 seasons at the club. He represented Norway in 67 internationals, scoring 23 times. He was honoured with an order of chivalry in his home country of Norway.

Summary: Ole Gunnar Solskjaer was well known as being the 'super-sub' and the 'baby-faced assassin'. He was regularly one of the club's top goalscorers until injuries blighted him in his final four years. After retirement, he managed the reserve team before taking over as first-team manager in 2018 until his dismissal in 2021. He is an extremely popular figure amongst the Old Trafford faithful.

NOBBY STILES

Born: 18th May 1942
United Debut: 1960
Nationality: English
Position: Midfielder
Height: 5 ft 6 in (1.68 m)
Major Trophies: 6

Early Career

Norbert Peter Stiles was born in the cellar of the family home during a WWII air raid in the area of Collyhurst in Manchester. He supported United growing up and played for the England schoolboys aged 15. He became an apprentice at the club in September 1957 and made his first team debut in October 1960 against Bolton Wanderers. He was also competing for the youth team at the time. Stiles netted his first goal three weeks later in his fourth game. He had his best scoring tally in his second season with seven goals.

Later Career

He won the First Division title with the club in 1965, playing in 41 of the 42 league games, and a personal best 59 games in all that season. He made his debut for the England national team in the same year versus Scotland, before scoring the only goal against West Germany in February 1966 at Wembley; his one and only goal for his country. A few months later he was a part of the squad that took part in the 1966 World Cup hosted by England. He played in every single game during the competition and was highly praised for his man-marking of the dangerous forward Eusebio in the semi-final win over Portugal. The England team won the tournament by beating West Germany in the final. He faced Eusebio again in the 1967/68 European Cup final when

United became the first English club to win in the European competition. They beat Benfica 4-1 that day. Stiles had triumphed with his second league winner's medal the season before. He played another 56 games in the 1968/69 season. Two seasons later, he played in his final game for the club in April 1971. Stiles was sold to Middlesbrough for £20,000 where he spent two seasons in the Second Division before making his final move to Preston North End in 1975. He took up football management after retiring, managing at former club Preston, the Vancouver Whitecaps and West Brom. Between 1989 and 1993, he was the Manchester United youth team coach, guiding trainees such as David Beckham, Ryan Giggs, and Paul Scholes through the ranks. In 2000, Stiles received an MBE in a belated achievement to honour his World Cup triumph with the England.

Accomplishments

Stiles played a total of 395 matches for Manchester United scoring 19 goals. He had 17 goals in 311 league matches in 11 seasons. His main honours included the First Division title twice, the European Cup once, and the FA Cup once. For England, he won 28 caps and recorded one goal. He was a member of the triumphant 1966 World Cup-winning team. He was honoured with an MBE in 2000 and inducted into the English Football Hall of Fame in 2007.

Summary: Nobby Stiles was one of English football's well known and most popular characters. With his missing teeth and short-sightedness, he was noted for his ball gaining and retention abilities. He passed away in October 2020. He is one of only three Englishman to win the World Cup and European Cup.

TOMMY TAYLOR

Born: 29th January 1932
United Debut: 1953
Nationality: English
Position: Forward
Height: 5 ft 11 in (1.80 m)
Major Trophies: 4

Early Career

Thomas Taylor was born in the small village of Smithies in Yorkshire. He left school at the age of 15, and started to play for a local coal mining team. In 1949, Taylor was signed by the local side Barnsley of the Second Division. He made his debut in October 1950, before proceeding to strike a hat-trick in his second professional game nearly a month later. He scored seven goals in 12 games during the season. After three seasons with the club, scoring 26 league goals in 44 matches, Taylor attracted the attentions of First Division champions Manchester United and he was transferred to the club in March 1953. He was one of the most expensive British footballers at the time, going for the unusual sum of £29,999. Matt Busby did not want to burden the 21-year-old Taylor as being a "£30,000 player", so he took a £1 note from his wallet and handed it to the lady who had been serving tea during the negotiations.

Later Career

Taylor scored two goals in his debut game for United a few days later, and ended the season with seven in his first 11 games. He had made his debut for the England national team two months after joining United. He was the club's top scorer the following season with 22 league goals in his first full season. This included two hat-tricks and two goals in a game three times. He was the joint top league goal scorer for the club in 1954/55. He won his maiden First Division title in the 1955/56 season by a margin of 11 points over the second-placed team. Taylor again impressed with 25 goals in the league, scoring in five consecutive games. The following season saw more of the same as United successfully defended their league title and reached the semi-finals of the European Cup competition at their first attempt. Taylor had a career-best season with 34 goals in 45 outings, including 22 in the league and eight in eight games in Europe. He struck two goals in a game six times during the title run and he bagged a goal in the FA Cup final. He belted a hat-trick in the record 10-0 demolition of Anderlecht and then scored in four successive matches in the quarter-final and semi-final ties in the European Cup. Taylor tragically passed away at the scene of the Munich air disaster when the plane returning from the European Cup game in Belgrade accidentally crashed on take-off in February 1958. He was just 26 years old.

Accomplishments

Taylor made 166 league appearances for United, scoring a remarkable 112 goals. He netted a total of 131 in 191 matches for the club. He was a member of the team that won two First Division titles. In 19 international games for England, he netted 16 goals - which remains one of the best goals to games ratio of any England international. He managed two hat-tricks for the team in the space of five months.

Summary: Tommy Taylor is regarded by those who saw him play as the greatest centre-forward ever to represent Manchester United and England. He has been described as the best header of a ball in his era and was so good that the great Alfredo Di Stefano of Real Madrid dubbed him 'Magnifico'. He had a plaque unveiled in Manchester where he used to stay.

NEMANJA VIDIĆ

Born: 21nd October 1981
United Debut: 2006
Nationality: Serbian
Position: Centre-back
Height: 6 ft 3 in (1.90 m)
Major Trophies: 15

Early Career

Nemanja Vidić was born in the town of Titovo Uzice in the former Yugoslavia. He started playing football at the age of eight for a local side. He then joined another team when 12. Before his 15th birthday, he was signed up by one of the top teams in Serbia, Red Star Belgrade to play in their youth system. Vidić played his first senior game for Spartak Subotica in 2000 whilst on loan. He was given the captaincy aged 20 and helped Red Star to a League and Cup double in 2004 before joining Russian side Spartak Moscow.

Later Career

After two seasons in Russia, Vidić signed for United in December 2005 for £7m and he made his debut in January. A month later, he won his first title with the club coming on as a late substitute in the League Cup Final. He formed a solid defensive partnership with Rio Ferdinand, and with 25 appearances, managed to win his first Premier League winner's medal in 2007. His first goal for the club had come in October. Two months later, he notched his first Champions League strike. Vidić obtained the Premier and Champions League double with the club the following season, including a man of the match performance in the Champions League Final. He was a part of the defence that kept 14 successive clean sheets in the League in 2008/09, as the club won its third consecutive title. He was named as the fans' player of the year at the end of the season. Vidić took over the captaincy role during the 2010/11 campaign and netted a goal in October that turned out to be the 1000th scored at Old Trafford in the Premier League. He got a vital goal against title-chasing Chelsea in May as United eventually went on to secure their fourth title in five years and a record-breaking 19th in the Premier League. He suffered some injury problems the following two seasons but managed to play over 20 league games in 2012/13 as he claimed his fifth League title with the club in seven years. Vidić eventually played his last game for United in May 2014, having scored in a Champions League quarter-final tie a month earlier. He left for Italian side Inter Milan and played one season for them before retiring in 2016. He is one of only three footballers to be honoured with the Player of the Season award in the Premier League twice alongside Thierry Henry and Cristiano Ronaldo.

Accomplishments

Vidić represented Manchester United in 211 league games and recorded 15 goals. In total, he played 300 times for the club. He won the Premier League five times, the Champions League once, and the League Cup three times with United. He won the League title once with Red Star Belgrade. He was Serbian Footballer of the Year twice. He played 56 times for the combined Serbia/Serbia and Montenegro/Yugoslavia teams scoring two goals. Vidić was part of Serbia and Montenegro's "Famous Four" defence that conceded just one goal during the ten 2006 FIFA World Cup qualification matches, setting a new record for the fewest goals conceded.

Summary: Nemanja Vidić was a no-nonsense hard man of a centre-back and serial winner of trophies in his nine seasons at the club. He is widely regarded as one of the Premier League's greatest centre-backs.

DENNIS VIOLETT

Born: 20th September 1933

Debut: 1953

Nationality: English

Position: Forward

Height: 5 ft 8 in (1.73 m)

Major Trophies: 2

Early Career

Born in the area of Fallowfield in Manchester, Dennis Sydney Viollet joined United in September 1949 as a youth team player. He worked through the junior ranks before becoming a professional a year later. He got his first senior game in April 1953 against Newcastle United. He then scored his first goal in his next game a week later. Viollet smashed in his first hat-trick in an amazing 6-5 victory versus Chelsea in October 1954. He netted the first goal of the game, and then United's fifth.

Later Career

He formed a forward striking partnership with Tommy Taylor, which helped United to the in 1956 league title. He got 20 league goals that season, having produced the same amount the previous year. Later on in the year, Viollet smashed four goals past Anderlecht in a European Cup game at Maine Road, the home of rivals Manchester City. He bagged three of those goals in the first half in the space of 14 minutes, before scoring the team's eighth with quarter of an hour to go. Taylor also got three goals in that game. He managed nine goals in the

European campaign as United reached the semis in their maiden outing in the competition, as the club retained the league title in the 1956/57 season. Viollet survived the Munich air disaster tragedy with mainly facial injuries. He competed with several new team members in the 1958/59 season and set a new club league record the following season with 32 goals in 36 games. He played his last game for his club in November 1961, scoring his final goal against Leicester City. In fact, he had scored in four of his last five matches for United. He had captured nine hat-tricks with the club in that time. All but five of his games had been played under the management of Matt Busby. After ten seasons with the club, Viollet was sold to Stoke City in early 1962 for £25,000 at the age of 28 where he played alongside the great Stanley Matthews. He scored 23 goals in his first full season and helped the club back to the First Division in 1963. He played his final game in 1970 and retired at the age of 36. After hanging up his boots, Viollet went to the United States and coached a variety of teams.

Accomplishments

Viollet appeared in 259 league games for United and scored 159 goals. In total, he played 293 times for the club and recorded 179 goals. He netted 20 goals or more in six consecutive seasons. There were 13 goals in 12 European games. He accumulated 225 league goals in 475 matches throughout his career. He won the First Division title on two occasions, both with United. He appeared twice for the England national team and scored once.

Summary: Dennis Viollet was one of the famed 'Busby Babes' and formed a formidable partnership with the more physical Tommy Taylor. He was noted for his pace and is joint fourth on United's all-time scorers list. He passed away in March 1999.

You have now come to the end of the book, I really hope you have enjoyed it and have learnt lots of awesome facts about these Manchester United legends to impress your mates and family.

As a small independent publisher, positive reviews left on our books go a long way to attracting new readers who share your passion for the game.

If you are able to take a few minutes out of your day to leave a review it would be greatly appreciated!

If you spot any issues you would like to raise, please do **email me before leaving a negative review** with any comments you may have.

I will be more than happy to liaise with you and can offer refunds or updated copies if you are unhappy with your purchase.

kieran.brown2402@gmail.com